T0159098

THIRD
WORLD WAR

DAVE RANKIN

authorHOUSE®

AuthorHouse™
1663 Liberty Drive
Bloomington, IN 47403
www.authorhouse.com
Phone: 1 (800) 839-8640

Painting on the front cover is called "The Mother" while on the back cover it is
called "The End of War". Both paintings on the cover are works of Dave Rankin.
Artworks or paintings used in this book are copyrighted to the author.

Published by AuthorHouse 01/14/2019

ISBN: 978-1-5462-7588-6 (sc)
ISBN: 978-1-5462-7590-9 (hc)
ISBN: 978-1-5462-7589-3 (e)

Library of Congress Control Number: 2019900239

Print information available on the last page.

This book is printed on acid-free paper.

CONTENTS

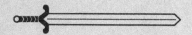

THE FERRYMAN

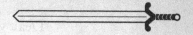

What's it like to have a war
Right there at your door
I'm not sure
That I can bring this to your shore
Across
The ocean of experience
That separates us
You from me
This sea
That stretches out
To infinity
It runs red
With the blood
Of all the dead
That i have walked over
Crawled across
Trampled on
And buried
It's scary
To even contemplate
Even telling you

Even describing to you
How the few
Of us
Who
Survived
Dealt with the remains
We're all insane
To one degree or another
But at least
We have each other
To tell our stories to
And be understood
But you'll never get it
No matter
How hard I try
No matter
How hard I cry
About all the arms and legs
And bodies like broken eggs
Shattered
My mind is battered
Just thinking about it
I mean
I have executed men
In cold blood
Put them to death
While you sat around
Smoking crystal meth

Or watching your tv
Waiting for the world to be
What you want
We are caught
In a dichotomy of worlds
And the river of sorrow
That separates us
This river of death
This river of loss
Can never be crossed
No matter what I say
Or how much I pay
The ferryman

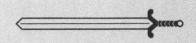

IT'S JUST A DREAM

It's just a dream
But it seems
So real
The feel
Of the rifle in my hands
The bands
Of fear
Strapped around my chest
It's a test
Of my psyche
This nightmare
That wakes me
From all the dead
It's all in my head
It's just a dream
But it seems
So real
The feel
Of the blood on my hands
The hot demands
Of the wounded

Crying out
I shout
In my sleep
It's just a dream
But it seems
So real
I feel
The screams
Cut through me
Like it was yesterday
Like it was last night
Like it just happened
My last firefight
And I'm still
Covered in blood
Lying in the mud
With my rifle in my hands
With my ammunition
At my side
Waiting for the tide
To turn
Waiting for the circle
To be complete
Waiting
For my last heartbeat
It's just a dream
But it seems
So real

And I feel
My sweat soaked sheets
Tied up around me
As I bend myself
Around this nightmare
It's just a dream
But it seems
So real
And I feel
So wrong
With my muddy bloody hands
Held so fiercely on my rifle
And I can't let go
Even though
I know
It's just a dream
But many times
It was real

EVERY NIGHT

Me
I watch a war
Every night in my mind
With my memory so unkind
I see the bombs and blood
I see the children die
And I see the mothers cry
And I don't wonder why
I return here
To this nocturnal melee
Ten thousand years of history
Have led me to this place
Where
The despondency and despair
Are haunting lessons
That no one's learned
From all the death
That's been earned
From all the fights
Battled thru the nights
From dusk to daylight

There are the screams
That wander thru my dreams
The wounded
Crying for their life
Amidst
All the surrounding strife
They howl and wail
For some relief
With some belief
That someone will save them

Those of us who survived
Were all revived
By the silence of the guns
The violence
That's been done
Appears slowly
With the rising sun
The bodies spread like eggshells
A thousand private hells
Displayed in the growing glare
A revelation
Of devastation
Upon a field once fair
To behold
In the early morning dawn
We all yawn
With tiredness
The bone deep fatigue

Of the sleep deprived
But we all strive
With adrenalin activated agility
The ability to continue
And finish all the work
Which none of us may shirk

This is how it starts
We pick up all the parts
While others dig a hole
Our goal
Is to bury all the bodies
But how gaudy
Is it
To collect
The pictures, weapons, pants and shirts
The rings and other things
That we take
Are enough to make
Even the hardest heart to break
The naked bodies
Go in the holes
And with our limbs and souls
All pained and hurt
We cover them with dirt
And walk away

Yet I stay
Every night

In this milieu
Asking what's my due?
What will I eventually pay
For having participated
In this direly dedicated
Destruction
The coin of my induction
Is that
I will always watch a war
Every night in my mind
Sometimes I wonder
If I'll ever find
Peace
Peace?
A little piece of me
Will always be buried
In that place
It's what I face
Every night
And when I've thought
I've left those things behind
Another war will start
Every night in my mind

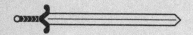

A Letter to Wanda

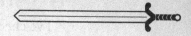

Dear Wanda
As I sit here
In this muddy hole
My memory
Takes its' toll
It's all I have
To keep my mind bent
Beyond the immediate
Environment
I think of you
In order to
Take my mind
Away
To stay
Sane
I need an anchor
Something
That will keep me
From the battle that will come
From the earsplitting hum
Of machine gun fire

Going to and fro
And so
I think of you
There's nothing else
That I can do
I've checked the weapons
I've checked the ammunition
I've checked our position
Our condition
Is all good
So while we wait
I think of you
It's true
I have other women
Nancy in Nanaimo
Hanna in Halifax
But I am halfway
Across the world
And facing
My mortality
Placing
In my mind
All my past
When I cast
My remembrance
Out like this
At this moment
Facing fate

I know
That it's too late
For you and I
But still
I think of you
All I can do
Is remember what was
Because
In the next few hours
Amongst the showers
Of mortar shells
And rushing gunmen
Some of them children
Perhaps I will not survive
My lapse
In judgement
In our relationship
Is my regret
And I cannot forget
Here at the end
And so
Wanda
I think of you

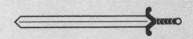

AROUND US

Motion churns
Around us
Violence burns
Around us
As the bullets fly
Around us
And the children cry
Around us
The mortars land
Around us
Our brothers scream
Around us
Death reigns
Around us
But we carry on
Around us
And they carry on
Around us
We fire
Around us
Killing them

Around us
Just as they kill us
And so it is
That war is thus
And it will not stop
Until we stop it
Around us

FEAR

I want you to imagine

Bullets flying past you

Hearing them sing

Their whining whimsical song

Passing through the air

Parting your hair

They're so close

To hitting you

What do you do

When you feel them go by

I can't lie

And say

I felt no fear

Because I lived it

I was scared to shit

Fear was a state

Of being

But the alternative

Was fleeing

From what we were seeing

In front of us

And that I could not do
I would rather die
Than be accused
Of being a coward
Of not having the balls
To fight
For something
I thought was right

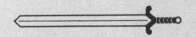

Dawn (Morning is Broken)

The sky is blue and beautiful

When dawn breaks

After battle

But every living heart aches

As the light reveals

The bloody broken ground

The bodies to be found

Between us and the treeline

There's no sound

Just a vacuum

Of stunned silence

After all the machinegunned violence

That raged throughout the dark

The scene is staged

For sunrise

For illumination

And no disguise

Can cover up

The slaughter

That surrounds us

All the dead

The end of all the lives they led
Are left on this field
In front of us
We're bereft
Because
So many of our own have died
On this field for which we vied
And created this carnage
That is so casually
Unveiled to our sight
In the early morning light

ECLIPSED

I killed someone today
And when I saw
His broken
Shattered body
Lying on the ground
I found
No satisfaction
My reaction
Was remorse
For him
For his family
For his wife
And children
He gave life
I didn't hate him
Or have anything
Against him
But I was told
To shoot him
He was the enemy
Did he want

Anything different from me?
I'll never know
Because now
He's a corpse
And the secrets
He may have told
Are gone
And dawn
Will not
Enlighten me
I will forever be
Eclipsed

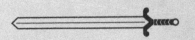

THE MOTHER

The echoes of her screams
Still ring in my ears
And I can hear
In my dreams
That ululating voice
Emanating pain
With no choice
But to evacuate
All her grief
In this sudden rush of sound
She's downed
She's on her knees
In the dirt
And her hurt
Hits me like a wall
She calls out to god
With her tortured soul
And a hole
Opens up inside of me
I will never be free
From the horror

Of her discovery
Her child
Her six year old son
Lying in the mud
With his blood
Pooled around his face
There is no grace
In this world
Of war and wantonness
There is only this
The death of innocence
And the agony
Of a mother's memory

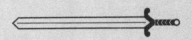

ANGUISH

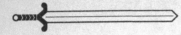

Anguish escapes
With immensity
And intensity
Pouring forth
In a vocal volcano
The pressure of the pain
Is unleashed
In a torrent of sound
Like a dam that breaks
And overflows
In an overwhelming scream
It seems
As though
The resonating sorrow
Cuts through
All who hear it
To be near it
When it discharges
The despondency and despair
Of the one afflicted
Is also to be inflicted

With all the fatal feelings
Of the one distraught
To be caught
In the oral agony
That deadly sonorous sea
Of sadness
And grief
Is but a brief
Reminder
To us all
An exposition
Of the thinness
Of our skin

THE COMMANDER

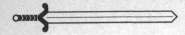

A hard man

With a hard job

I've never seen him flinch

In the face of danger

No stranger

To death is he

But in misery

He walks about

No smile ever on his face

And never

One thing out of place

His hat

His hair

His uniform

And rifle

One look from him

Will stifle

Any humour

There's a rumour

That goes around

That he has

Put in the ground
A thousand men
Children
He once had
And a wife
Who gave them life
Now all gone
They were lost
They were tossed
Into this war
And taken
Who knows how
Or in what kind
Of circumstance
By chance
The commander
He survives
He thrives
On his hatred
Of his enemies
At every turn
His concern
Is to defend us
So he tends us
Like a flock of sheep
He doesn't sleep
He patrols
Night and day

He controls
Everything
In every way
Not a heartbeat
Happens here
Of which he's not aware
His care
Comes casually
Almost callously
With disdain
But his pain
Is obvious
For those of us
Who choose to see
A man obsessed
With the memory
Of the family
He once possessed

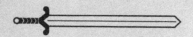

AK 47

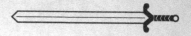

The AK 47
Mikhail Kalishnikov's invention
Is an assault rifle
Meant
To kill men
Created
For close combat
And for those of us
Who have done that
It's the most reliable weapon
In the world
It's curled
30 round magazine
Will never jam
And it's easy to load
And because of its' shape
You'll never be confused
Which way it goes
Even in the dark
It's not accurate very far
But its' bullets

Will go through a car
And hit someone hiding
On the other side
It can't be denied
That the walls of a building
Are no defense
Against this machine
Fired at close range
It's not strange
That something so
Deadly and devastating
Has been devised
By a humanity
So despised
By each other

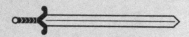

RIFLE MAINTENANCE

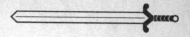

Clips and buttons
Triggers and springs
All the little
Mechanical things
That make a rifle work
Are so important
When your life
Depends on it
Which is why
We are constantly
Frantically
Frenetically
Taking them apart
And putting them
Back together again
With a bit of oil
Through the barrel
To ensure
The projectile
Will not jam
We do this

So many times

We can do it blind

In the dark

So that we won't

Miss our mark

When the time comes

To kill someone

Who wants

To kill us

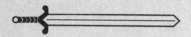

THRENODY

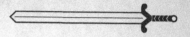

Perimeter mines
Announce the advance
Of our enemies
We don't know them
And they
Don't know us
But on this night
We will fight
To the death
No shot of crystal meth
Or line of cocaine
Will alter the brain
In the way
That incoming fire
Will charge the synapses
Momentary lapses
Will get you killed
Or worse
Your buddy beside you
Or the one behind
To be kind

We say
That death is random
While we try to fathom
Why him?
Why not me?
But we
We don't see
The pointlessness
What we see
Is an enemy
Killers
That must be
Put down
A burst of sound
From a mortar shell
Illuminates
This hell
Where we will survive
Or not
Ringing ears
And smoke stung tears
Isolate us
We are each
On our own
All our deaths
Will be alone
Tomorrow
With our sorrow

The crows will come

And the hum

Of flies

And the ravens' cries

Will compose

A dirge for the dead

A lamentation

A threnody

For what has occurred

For what both

The dead and the living

Have endured

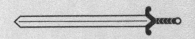

CHARLIE

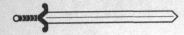

When I arrived
Charlie
Gave me
A flack jacket
We had to backpack it
200 miles
With only
A change of clothes
And a weapon
And ammunition
And nutrition
In the form
Of American army rations
The fashions
In the jungle
Might not extend
Beyond shorts
And a t-shirt
But if you're gonna fight
A flack jacket might
Be a good idea

And Charlie gave me one
Not quite done
He taught me to fight
And many nights
We fought side by side
The tide
Of battle
Finally turned
Against us
And Charlie
Standing in my place
Took a bullet
In the face
This strife
Took his life
Standing where I should be
And me
I just ruthlessly
Carried on fighting
But my ammunition
Ran out
And when an enemy fell in
To our position
I beat him to death
With my rifle
With my breath
In a panic
I was manic

And struck out blind
In the morning
I would find
What I had done
The commander came by
And asked me why
I was still huddled there
I didn't care
About the other guy
But about Charlie
And the fact
That I had smashed
His head in
In the melee
In the dark
When I couldn't see
And the commander said
"They're both dead.
Let's go have breakfast."

MERCY KILLING

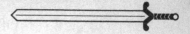

I saw the flash

Of the RPG

Leave the trees

It was directed

Directly

At our position

Supposition

Would be

That it hit us

But it passed

Right over us

And hit the hut

Of the woman

We were defending

No questions pending

I ran back

To rummage

Through the remains

Hoping to find

That someone survived

And I did

The baby lived
But the woman
And her four other kids
Were all done in
The sin
Of this murder
Was already
Being avenged
By the time
I realized
That the RPG team
Was compromised
By my brothers in arms
They had caught them
And held them down
Machetes came out
And without a doubt
The death of 1000 cuts began
And as I ran
To follow them
They started with their feet
It wasn't complete
When I got there
But it had gone
Far enough for me
I was horrified
My disgust
Could not be denied

And I knew these guys
Were the living dead
So I shot them
Both
In the head
By definition
This rendition
Is a war crime
But to me
At the time
It was not vengeance
It was not execution
It was mercy killing

THE MEDIC

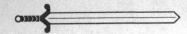

Today
Is just like
Any other day
But I don't
Feel that way
I feel the loss
I feel the cost
Of the wars I've fought
I'm definitely not
Overwhelmed by this
I actually miss
The combat
Because it was important
For the people we defended
And the wounded that I mended
Acting as a medic
In my mind
The flares still shine
On the bodies
With the glare
Reflecting from fresh blood

Incoming fire
Flashes my desire
To help those downed
Screaming for their lives
Each of us strives
To do our best
And this was a test
That pushed me
To my limits
And I feel I failed
My brothers in arms wailed
While I tried to reach them
To try to save them
But I couldn't
Not because I wouldn't
I did
I never hid
From enemy fire
I shot them as I ran
I made a stand
To save my brothers
And others died
As my brothers cried
With wounds from bullets
And shrapnel
What the hell
Are we doing here
I was so near

But couldn't reach them
In time
So we covered them
With lime
The next morning
And my mourning
Will never cease
I will never be at peace

LIFEBLOOD

In my memory
Red hot blood
Floods
Over my hands
As I try
To staunch the flow
Gushing
And rushing
From what's left
Of my buddy's leg
Blown off
By a mortar shell
His left leg
Is almost gone
Right up to the hip
And I dip
My fingers
Into the remaining part
Trying to find
The artery
That's severed

I will never
Forget the panic
That overcame me
While his life
Flowed
Over my hands
And I remember
The look in his eye
That said
Don't even try
And with the slightest shake
Of his head
He was gone
He was dead
And I sat there
Drenched
In his lifeblood
My mind
Totally wrenched
With guilt
And grief
My belief
In any kind
Of higher power
Gone
Taken away
Stolen
In that moment

When he died
I could have cried
In that moment
But I didn't
I screamed

MY RIFLE

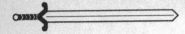

I had a rifle
Put in my hands
And I was told
How to use it
I had a rifle
Put in my hands
And I was told
"Don't lose it"
I had a rifle
Put in my hands
And I was told
When the time comes
You'll know
What to do with it
And sure as shit
The time came
And I knew
What to do
I counted rounds
That I fired
I never tired

Of switching magazines
With my buddy
Beside me
Trading and taking turns
At firing
One night us two
We went through
14 boxes
Of ammunition
Perdition
Damnation
And ruination
Wait for us
Because that night
In that fight
We counted
Forty men
That we killed
If I was to build
A monument
For the men who died
By my hand
It couldn't be grand
Enough
To console myself

For them
Or their families
But it wasn't me
That killed them
It was my rifle

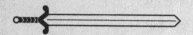

CAMOUFLAGE

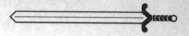

I see my face
All in camouflage
Too late
I contemplate
What I'm doing
Why I'm here
Who is this person?
This reflection in front of me
This guerilla
That I see?
There's an emptiness
In those eyes
That no amount of paint
Will disguise
There's a hardness
And a resignation
I don't need imagination
To understand these things
The image brings
About the knowledge
That this is

A commercially contrived war
But what we struggle for
Is simply survival
For a handful
Of simple people
Who only want
To live their lives in peace
To watch their children grow
And see the seeds they sow
All come to maturity
Instead
We witness
While
They're all mown down
Trampled to the ground
I ask the mirror
For a reason
For a rationale
Something
Anything
That might explain
This insane
Combat that we fight
Foresight
Should have warned me
But I didn't realize
And now
I don't recognize

The person I've become
The camouflage is permanent
And I hide
Inside of it
From all the horror
From all the stench
From all the blood
That flowed
I'm not owed anything
And I have paid
In my own way
For my participation
There's no disgrace
In the colours on my face
But even when
I'm all washed clean
Those colours
Can still be seen

THE SONG – DOWN AND OUT

I didn't feel the bullet
That put me down
Lying on the ground
Seeing my blood
Flood from my chest
I knew
That it was best
Just to say my prayers
And be thankful
For the life I had
It wasn't bad
This acceptance of death
It was certainly
A surprise
When I saw
My next sunrise
And I was quite sure
That I could endure
The pain
But I was wrong
It was a song

That sang thru me
In every key
Like I was
A multiple tuning fork
I learned to laugh at it
But every time I moved
It resonated in my bones
It followed me
Whereever I went
It was a song
That was sent
From hell
And in my mind
I burned
While my brain turned
Those last moments
Over
And over
And over
A memory rover
I became
Living the very same
Seconds
After I fell
I now know very well
That I was not confused
In those moments
Before passing out

There was no doubt
That it was a child
Who shot me
And I could see
That someone shot him
As my sight got dim
We made eye contact
Both downed
Both
Lying on the ground
Both
Wondering
How we got here
And even after 20 years
Even tho it's been so long
I can still hear
That same old song

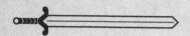

BROTHERS

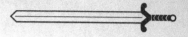

Days on days
One so much
Like the other
My brothers
We sleep
We wake
How much can we take
We struggle through
The winter winds
And suffer under
The summer sun
We have fun
With our dark
Sarcastic humour
A good rumour
Is like lightening
Through our ranks
Our banks
Might be full
But we're never home
And I could write a tome

Filled with airports
And planes
And sites
Where we fight
Every day
Where we find
Another way
To continue
To accomplish
A purpose
Dictated
By governments
And companies
Who care nothing
For our lives
We survive
In spite of them
And I know
And really think
That even
Our weakest link
Is my brother
Like no other
We have shared
Sweat and tears and blood
And pissing on your feet
In order to treat
Athlete's foot

We've seen each other injured
And some of us die
In the most horrible ways
And those memories stay
With us
We are brothers
To this day
And no others
Can share
With us
Our experience
The drama
The trauma
That we went through
"We few
We happy few
We band of brothers"

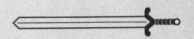

PERSPECTIVE

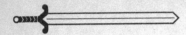

You think you know me
But the intricacy
Of my psyche
Is beyond any conception
Of reality
You may have seen
Where I have been
Is outside the box
And like different socks
We clash in colour
Even tho the cloth
Is the same
Our aim
Beneath the dye
Runs a common weave
We believe
Similar things
But our pasts
Have cast
Different moulds in our thinking
Where yours is conformed

To western mediocre
Mine is deformed
By the streets
And by war
My core
Was irrevocably changed
My mind deranged
By blood and body parts
Poverty and starvation
Deprivation on a massive scale
Throughout the world
While you live in privilege
With a superficial knowledge
Of those who suffer
Or do without

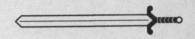

I HUNG A FLOWER

I hung a flower

Today

From a piece of barbed wire

Because I've been under fire

From those

Who

Would take away freedom

I hung a flower

Today

From a piece of barbed wire

Because I admire

All those

Who

Have stood up with me

For the right to be free

For the right

To express themselves

As they see

Fit

I hung a flower

Today

From a piece of barbed wire
Because it's my desire
That no one
Should suffer
The depression
Of oppression
To have their existence
Obfuscated
Or negated
By the powers that be
And so I quietly
Hung a flower
Today
From a piece of barbed wire
Hoping
That I'll inspire
Others to believe
That we can achieve
A state of peace
That we can cease
Destroying ourselves
And each other
I can't smother
My feelings about this
And so
I hung a flower
Today
From a piece of barbed wire

Hoping to light a fire
In the hearts
Of those who listen
Of those who take heed
That there is a need
In this world
To stop the greed
To stop the aggression
To stop the repression
And give voice
To self expression
I hung a flower
Today
From a piece of barbed wire
Because i aspire
To a reality
That does not include barbarity

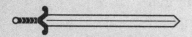

ANGRY SARCASTIC ASSHOLE

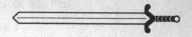

I've met some people
Who understand me
Who know
What it's like to be
A war vet
And then
Everyone else I've ever met
Thinks I'm an angry sarcastic asshole
But I was just reassured today
That in my way
I'm a nice asshole...
Because i say please....
As in
Please go fuck yourself....
Or...
Please fuck off and die...
Or please...
Let the next bus hit you...
It's true
Because that's nice...
It's polite...

Like please take my gun
From its' shelf
And go shoot yourself...
And i'd say thank you afterwards
But that would be a waste of breath
Cuz your death
Would make it pointless
And the point of this message
Is that
Yes I am an angry sarcastic asshole
You don't even know the half
And I'm having a good laugh
Even writing this...
The world as i i've seen it
Ain't the white washed
9 to 5
Picket fence
Pay cheque on Friday
With two point two kids
And a minivan....
It ain't soup in a can
Or jam in a jar
It's Myanmar
And Angola
It's ebola and HIV
The world I see
Has dead bodies
And bullet counts

Founts of blood
And flares at night
It has gun fights
And torture and rape
It has no red tape
Just violence and hate
And enough other shit
To fill the reservoir
Of the Hoover Dam....
God damn
Yes i'm angry
And sarcastic
And I'm an asshole...
Because if you don't know enough
To pick up behind yourself
And don't know enough
To do what you do properly
And don't know enough
To have some respect for other people
Even if they don't know....
Yes i will be angry...
And i will be sarcastic....
And you will perceive me as an asshole...
Because you are an asshole
And should be treated as such
And i don't care that much
What you think
Cuz i won't sink

Into a world

That makes martyrs

Over religion

Or that barters over

Human flesh

Or that weaves a mesh

To bind us all

Into a long suffering hell

I know pretty well

Who I am

I'm an angry

Sarcastic

Asshole

But I'm a nice asshole

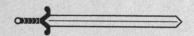

Right and Wrong

I wanna tell a tale of war
I wanna tell a story
About humanity
Once upon a time
I fought a war
In fact
I fought the same war
Twice
The first time
I was wounded
In the back of my head
I thought that I was dead
When the mortar fragment
Caught me from behind
And brought me oblivion
And unconsciousness
The second time
I was shot in the chest
And then
I really thought
It was the end

But I awoke
To all the smoke
And mirrors
Played out
By politicians
And the corporeal
Corporate technicians
Who play so many games
With so many
Different aims
With so many lives
Held
In their hypothetical hands
It stands
To reason
That I would return
And fight again
I was young
And energetic
I had a cause
And I didn't pause
After my recovery
I went back
Because
I didn't lack
In the courage
To stand and fight
One may ask

Who was right?
But I don't know
And probably never will
However
I do know
Who
Was
Wrong

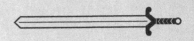

COMMUNICATION

Talk to me

Please

Put me at ease

Because I will never get

On my knees

For anything

They can shoot me first

Or they can bring devastation

To those I know

But into submition

I will not go

Talk to me

Return me

Or help me to return

To fields that don't burn

With anticipatory hatred

The inbred

Desire

To seek out annihilation

Of those

Who don't even stand

In the way
I can't say
Where I've been
What I've seen
It's all an allusion
To what we call
The real world
Like a flag unfurled
Reality flaps
And snaps
In whatever way
The most powerful hands
In any lands
May direct it
Or correct it
With a brutish coercion
Or the thoughtless profusion
Of accumulated wealth
All acquired
With the stealth
Of a cat in the night
Marking it's territory
Everybody's story
Like a great big
Pissing contest
With the smell
To judge
Who's best

The real test
Will come with time
Like the lime
Buried in the graves
Of all those who fought
Never having learned
The lessons taught
By the romans
The greeks
Chinese
British empire
Bonaparte
None can stand apart
And witness Stalingrad
As a battle of the wits
Everyone froze their tits
In a wasteland of factories
And forced confrontation
Yet still we pursue
A death that's undue
For the young
For the naieve
For those who believe
In a better condition
For the human race
A disgrace
For those who stand to the side
And there abide

In patterns of living
Not worth giving
The effort to defend
Those who's end
Is perfectly defensible
Reprehensible
This neglect
To which
I'm able to connect
By marks made permanent
Upon the firmament
Of my body
Our shoddy
Sociological care
For our fellows as a species
Make me desire to deliver feces
Because endlessly
Humanity
Deserves
Shit

WHY WE FIGHT

Our history is fraught
With all the wars
That have been fought
In the name of religion
Or politics
But the idea that sticks
In my mind
Is commerce
Not a single war
Has happened in our history
Where the goal
Was not control
Of some resource
What recourse
Do we have
Against the tide
Of those with wealth
Only wanting more
Who with their stealth
Obscure their aims

Behind all the political games
That are manifested
In our media
For money
And for power
They polish their policies
Pollute our planet
And our minds
They instigate
And obfuscate
They dictate
And regulate
They manipulate
Us
Into thinking
That they're right
This
Is why we fight

HUMAN HISTORY

Human history
Is a story of war
And all the gore
Left on the battlefields
That the birds picked clean
From which we could glean
So much about the reasons
Throughout 10000 seasons
And so many more
Why humans went to war
Greed, envy, jealousy
Territory and control
I can extol
A myriad of purpose
To pursue this deadly game
Fortune and fame
Or just to kill or maim
Another man to prove you can
More prevalent
And more evident

Is the essence of our economies
And still societies
Abound
In which it's found
That glorious death can be had
Religious jihad
Is nothing different
From any other confrontation
Throughout our past
The last 5000 years
Has been a waste of time
Technology, philosophy and science
Have not helped us
In advancing
The pharoah's horses are still prancing
In the harness that they wore

WAR AND PEACE

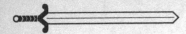

The deeds I've done

Lie heavy in my chest

As my scars can attest

The deformed tissue

Caused

By Russian issue

Ammunition

There's no contrition

That I can see in this reflection

These marks on my body speak to me

In the mirror

And in all the casual gestures

Like running my fingers thru my hair

Or scratching the hole in my chest

And with no amount of alliteration

Can I allude

To any frame of state

Where I can delude

Myself from these facts

With no amount of tact

Can I tiptoe

Around this reality
That I bear physically
I scratch my chest
Run my fingers thru my hair
And I don't dare
To deny
The things that I
Have helped happen
My innocence was stolen
By the death of others
Were they my brothers?
On the other side of that field
To their tide we did not yield
And I don't care
What others think
About this past
That I carry
And attempt to convey
Because we stood fast
And because
Now at last
I've found the freedom
For which I fought for others
I have found my escape
I have found my release
I have found
My own form
Of peace

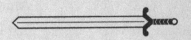

THE WARRIOR'S LAMENT

This is for all of those
Who fought and died
Even more
For those who survived
And lived to tell the tales
That live with us today
Come what may
There are those of us
Who will fight
And we will sacrifice
Everything we hold dear
To protect those that we hold near
From tyranny
From despotism
To protect those we love
The people that we know
Allowing liberty
In the face of mortal danger
We become a stranger
To those who think
That they know us

When we no longer

Know ourselves

There are shelves

In our minds

Where we place

These memories

A space

Where we contain

The remains

Of all the battles fought

The opposites

Of things we were taught

When we were young

And innocent

With no thought

About mortality

And the questions

That it brings

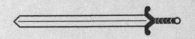

GUILT

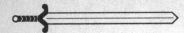

The things
That I have seen
In the places
I have been
Are no where
That you want to go
But I want you to know
About them anyway
Back in the day
When I fought my war
I swore
To defend the innocent
I spent
A year and a half
With a gun in my hand
Making a stand
With a bunch
Of other mercenaries
To protect
A bunch
Of people

That none of us knew
But we grew
Together
Through all the battles
Through all the fights
Fought through all the nights
The mornings dawning
With carnal chaos yawning
In front of us
And behind
Fate was kind
To some of us
We survived
We weren't deprived
Of limbs or lives
But others were
And I can't cure
The guilt
Of failure
The feeling
That we could have
Done more for
Those who didn't make it
Somedays

I can't take it
But today
I am able to care
Enough to share
My guilt
With you

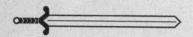

REGRET

My heart

Goes out

Without a doubt

To those

I have left behind

In my mind

It's an imposition

To share

My past laid bare

Like a wasteland

Exposed

To the sun

What fun

Is it

For those I hold dear

To hear

These stories

Of death

And devastation

A path

Of blood and gore

Things that I
Cannot ignore
But what
Makes it necessary
That they should hear
To participate
In this past
To take on my memories
And hold them as their own
I cannot condone
Such a sharing
But I am not beyond caring
About what I've done

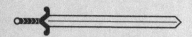

INNOCENCE DIES

Innocence always dies
It always does
It's not because
It can't live
I would give
Anything
For it to go
On and on
But innocence will die
That's a for sure
None of us is pure
It'll happen from blood
Or bad behavior
Or from the flavour
Of ice cream
That tastes wrong
So sing a song
And make it good
Because I know I would
I'm at an age
Where my pen

On the page
Makes me tired
Of trying to understand
That my hand
Won't make a difference
Innocence will die
And I refuse to cry
About it anymore
I can only be there
To share
In the disappointment
When life
Doesn't do
What we expect it to

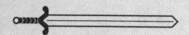

REFLECTION

I sit
At an empty table
Near the window
Of the café
By my place
Inside
It is calm
And the customers
Are courteous
Outside
The wind howls
In its' fury
Forcing snowflakes
Into a driving whirlwind
Which I watch
As the dervishes dance
Up and down the street
A good day to meet
Anyone
Conversations in Canada
Being so easily

Initiated
By weather
I greet and meet
Numerous escapees
From the storm
We all laugh
But they don't know half
Of what I'm thinking
In comparison
This conflagration
Is a pale shade
Of where I've been
I don't judge them
But my reflection
In the window
Shows a man
Who has seen too much
And can never
Really share
Because most "them"
Don't care
The storm of my life
Has frozen me
In a solitary state
Where my memories
Are the mirrored walls
Keeping me in

FORTUNE

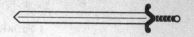

Fortune
Has smiled on me
Many times
My many crimes
Were weft
Into the weave
Of balance
Now I'm left
With the chance
To achieve
Some meaning
Something less unseeming
Than what has gone before
I cannot ignore
The history I have led
The innocence
That I have pled
Is marred
By my choices
The voices
From my past

Deny
My liberty
They do not
Set me free
They challenge me
To make things straight
To make things right
I can't
"sit tight"
As if nothing has occurred
I'm not innured
To the emotions
Of the dead
No matter what I've pled
They
Are
All
Still
Dead
And I
I am still here
To set things straight
To set things right
To set the balance
To set the scales
To stop the pendulum
From swinging
To raise the singing

For those
Whose fortune
Found me lacking
For those
I could not protect
For those
I could not shelter
From the storm
Or
For those
That necessity made me kill
The thrill
Was only survival
All in all
Fortune
Or not

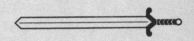

HAPPINESS IS

I've been accused

Of being happy

Like happiness was a disease

Of course I'm happy

I'm alive

I've survived

Two wars

I'm a combat vet

And yet

I'm happy

I hate broccoli

And traffic

And politics

But I ignore that shit

I'm even entertained by it

I've been dead twice

But I'm still alive

So yeah

I'm happy

And if you have an issue with that

Well I have a tissue

Just for you
To wipe your eyes
Because I have cried
So many tears
For everyone I've seen die
And I'm not done with it
So I always have
A little bit of tissue
Or napkin
Or something
To wipe my eye
But I'm happy
Cuz I'm alive
I survived

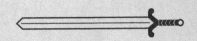

I CAN'T RELAX

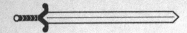

Do I have something to say?
Yeah
I got something to say
And there ain't no way
They're gonna shut me up
Or shut me down
And you can frown
All you like
Cuz I ain't no clown
Here to make you smile
That ain't my style
Far from it
So I'm gonna stand
On the summit
Of my soapbox
And I'm gonna have my say
I'm gonna show you the way
That I fight my war
Let you know what I struggle for
You have my word
That I aim to be heard

So my opinions
Are not rendered toothless
By all the truthless media
Screaming in our ears
And all those ruthless
Politicians out there
Trying to feather their own beds
Letting power go to their heads
While people are homeless
And kids are crying
Cuz they're hungry
And people are dying
In armed conflicts
For corporate greed
I will not cede
A single centimeter
Of the ground I'm standing on
This ain't some square
I just landed on
In some cosmic game of chance
This ain't no romance
When there's millions
Of women and children
Being sold into sexual slavery
Where's the bravery
To stand up against this
Did I miss
Something here

I don't know
And so
I'll just keep
Piecing together my poems
Word by word
Sentence by sentence
And rhyme by rhyme
Cuz it's about time
That we realize
That racism is a crime
Against people
We don't even know
And what do we have
To show for it
Nothing but violence and hate
But it's not too late
To change things
And it's not too late
To finally admit
That homosexuality
Is a reality
And that nothing
Anyone can say
Will change the way
That people love each other
So I'm gonna continue
Speaking my mind
In every venue

I can find
Until these things start changing
I'm gonna keep rearranging
My message
Word by word
Phrase by phrase
And I know days
That I despair
But I know
There's people out there
Who listen
Who know my mission
About liberty
And what it means to be free
And that this is a war
And I fight it with words
And I can't relax
Til I know I've been heard

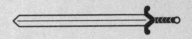

Rise Up Now

Blood glints
In the light
From the flares
The shine of it hints
At the damage
That's been done
We haven't won
Yet
But we will
In the end
Our job to defend
This place
And these people
No questions asked
We've been tasked
To fight the enemy
To the death
And whether
It's ours
Or theirs
Doesn't matter

Although the latter
Is preferable
But we don't care
Because we dare
To stand up
And fight repression
Overt aggression
Announced by landmines
Going off in the dark
Who amongst you would hark
To this call?
Be willing to fall
For a principle?
It's pretty simple
We are all equal
We all have a right
To our beliefs
It doesn't matter
What colour we are
It doesn't matter
Who we choose to love
We should be above
All of that
Killing my fellow man
Is not fun
But no one
Should be oppressed
Because of how they're dressed

Or for any other reason
No one's will
Should be imposed
On another
And those who try
Should be opposed
And so
There is nothing
That I will not do
In order to
Protect you
And your right to be free
For your right to be
Who you are
Who amongst you
Would go so far
As to stand with me
Because the time has come
To rise up now

DEFENSE OF INNOCENCE

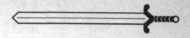

Most people
Who physically hurt
Someone else
Who cause
Another person pain
Most people
Who do this
Will be shocked
By what they've done
But not me
My official body count
Is 43
Which means
That I have probably killed
Around 90 men
I've buried
A thousand bodies
And all those men
That I killed
All deserved it
I have no qualms

About violence
Because I won't stand
Violation
Of anyone's rights
I won't stand down
And I won't stand back
I will go on attack
When I hear
Or see
Something wrong
How I long
To be back
In a war zone
Where I could be free
To be the real me
The guy
Who could casually
Kill someone
For raping a child
Or beating a woman
Or stealing a crust of bread
From someone with nothing
Dead
Is how that ends
It all depends
On the situation
The real me
This person that you see

Right here
And right now
Will defend you
In any way
Shape or form
That I can
Because I'm a man
That sees the world
The way it should be
I'm a man who knows
What it means to be free
Because I'm a man
Who knows that
Innocence needs to be
Protected
Because I'm a man
Who knows
That just because
You think differently from me
Doesn't mean
That you have any less
Hope in your heart
Or blood in your body
Or sanctity
In your soul
And it doesn't mean
That you should be scared

To defend yourself
But maybe
You don't need to
Because there are people like me
Who will do it for you

WHY WERE YOU THERE?

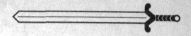

Why were you there?
I've been asked
Like I've been tasked
With an exercise
Of justification
For what I've done
And there are none
That I've known
That could have shown me
A different path
From the bloodbath
That I've seen
The repression
And oppression
There is no suggestion
That can make this question
Stand up
To any
Kind of scrutiny
Under my eye
Why were you there?

For what reasons
For those seasons
Did I give my life
For those
Who could not
Defend themselves
On what shelves
Should I put
The files
That record
A different history
Where I didn't
Make that stand
It wasn't planned
But it wasn't like
I could choose
I'm glad I did
Because I never hid
From doing what I should
And what good
Would have been accomplished
Another way
And every day
When they say
Why were you there?
I feel despair
For those I have witnessed die
I still cry

After all these years
For things my peers
Can never understand
And there's a band
Running through me
A stripe of sorrow
Black
Against the white
Of tomorrow
The shiny bright
Hope
For the future
It's how I cope
It's what I covet
And have to believe
Why were you there?
They ask
Why did you dare
To tempt
Any accident of fate
And I respond
That my date
With death
Was predetermined
And is undetermined
By any conscious
Choice of mine
There's only so much time

That's been given
To each of us
And I won't make a fuss
If I go down
Defending others
I won't frown
At the end
That I fought
For what was right
Why were you there?
Everyone asks
Except the children
Where have you been?
Is their question
Where have you been?
The children ask
No where
That you ever wanna be
No where
You should ever have to see
That's where I've been

WAR DIDN'T KILL ME

War didn't kill me
But it surely took my life
The one I knew
All the strife
Has broken me
Do you really want to see
All my scars
The keloid mars
That have been left
On my body
In my soul
And in my mind
The amount of metal
Pulled from this shell
So I could
Survive in it
Less complete
Than I was before
Replete
In the understanding
And maybe more

Maybe I grew
From this invasion
Of machine guns
And mortars
And landmines
And phosphorous flares
The broken bodies
And bloody ground
The limbs to be found
Separated from their owners
All the burnt remains
All that I retain
In my memory
Maybe made me
More than less
I confess
That I am broken
This is not a token
Confession
I AM broken
War didn't kill me
But it took
The life I knew
And it made me
Look at all of you
Very differently

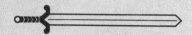

HOW THE WORLD WORKS

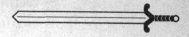

"Why did you never
Say anything about this?"
People ask
Well
I have to tell
That no one knew
Where I was
And that's because
I travelled the world
Freelance
Not saying a word
No one having heard
Anything from me
For months or years
And when I came back
After what I'd been thru
Who
Do you think
That I would tell
About my own private hell
Exposed

Like the decomposed
Bodies
Lying out there
Waiting to be buried
Wafting noxious fumes
Who would want
To exhume
Those memories
And why should I be
Required
To give in
To this desire
To confess
I will profess
That I know more
About the world
Than most people I've met
And it ain't pretty
Don't have pity
For me
For what I've experienced
All the death
And destruction
And all the hate
It's too late
For you to anticipate
Feeling magnanimous
Because it's just us

Here right now
And I can't tell you how
It opened my eyes
To all the lies
If you
Only knew
How the real world operates
You would be scared
To death
It would take your breath
Away to see
The mayhem
And murder
And torture
And rape
Your mouth would gape
In fear
And wonder
At this world
Torn asunder
By greed
And plunder
"Why did you never
Say anything about this?"
I didn't say
Anything before
Because war
Happens each

And every day
And you all pay
For it to happen
With your taxes
And your ignorance
You've built a fence
To keep out reality
And you would deny me
And turn me off
Like your TV
When you didn't want to hear
What I have to say
About the way
The world really works

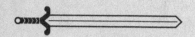

WE WILL FIGHT

My official body count
Is 43
If it were up to me
It'd be
Zero
I'm no hero
But I will stand and fight
For what I believe
And to relieve
People that I know
I will go
Into enemy fire
No matter how dire
The situation
Capitulation
Is not a question
There is no turning back
And there is no running away
There is no giving up
And putting your hand in the air
Don't you dare

Put down your gun
Every second
Every minute
Every hour
Of every day
We will fight
In every way
We can
And I will stand
Beside you
And we will fight
Yes we will fight
Against things that aren't right
We will fight against abuse
I know you're not obtuse
I know you can see
The way things SHOULD be
And so we will fight
Against fascists
And sexists
And racists
And rapists
We will fight
Against pedophiles
We will even fight
Against fashion styles
We will fight
For the poor

We might not win
But we will endure
And we will fight
And we might
Not win
And that's not the end
That I'd be picking
But believe you me
We will
Go down kicking

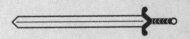

STRAIGHT WHITE MALE

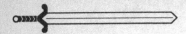

When I was young
I went and fought
For something I believed in
Because I was taught
That everyone has value
I don't care what hue
Your skin is
And I don't care what you do
In the privacy of your bedroom
And I don't care who you worship
Or what you believe
I will not deceive you
When I say
As long as you don't judge me
I won't judge you
My die has been cast
My plaster has been set
I'm a battle hardened
Combat vet
And I've been spit on
And spat at

For that
It ain't nice
But it's the price
I pay
For being who I am
A warrior
A widowmaker
A lifetaker
A groundshaker
For those who would not
Or could not
Defend themselves
I have sacrificed
I have been dead twice
I have had
Enough metal
Pulled from my body
To make this microphone stand
Yet still
I would give a helping hand
To anyone
Who asked me nice
I have fought
Tooth and nail
For every pail
Of sand
To create my castle
On the beach

Just out of reach

Of those who would judge me

Because I'm male and straight and white

Well I might be white

And male and straight

But I do not participate

In hate

Except to confront it

And to kill it

And fuck everybody

Who looks at me

And thinks differently

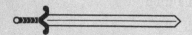

SELFISHNESS

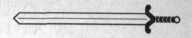

I sit here listening
To all the glowing grammar
That pours forth
And I won't stammer
When I tell you
That I think to myself
I must be in the land of Oz
Everyone has a cause
I mean
Let's take a pause
And think about this
Did I miss
Something
Along the way
Like I don't care
If you're gay
It doesn't interest me
And stolen land
Is a fact of history
Everyone here is a victim
And everyone here

Is descended from a thief
It's my belief
That we're all guilty
Of one serious thing
And that's ignorance
And I don't care to hear
Your defense
I don't have the time
When only 29
Out of 1000
Sexual assaults
Are recorded as a crime
12 have charges laid
And only 3 are made
To pay
While 997 assailants
Walk away free
It seems to me
That we
Have bigger problems
More basic problems
Than pipelines
Or parking fines
If you want to be bold
Look at the world
Because I am told
That 2 million women are sold
Every year

Into sexual slavery
And you want to be free
To hug fucking trees
Or wear women's clothes
Or bung up your nose
With cocaine
Are you fucking insane?
Or is it just me?
I mean
I don't care what you do
But I don't want to be
The one who tells you
That every 15 minutes
Of every day
Someone is killed
Or maimed in some way
By a landmine
Left lying in wait
For their date
With fucking fate
The worst areas
Of the world
Are Afghanistan
Angola
Cambodia
Iraq
And Laos
But also

Bosnia
Croatia
Georgia
Mozambique
And Myanmar
Nicaragua
Somalia
Sri Lanka
And the Sudan
You can't plan
In these places
To go for a casual stroll
because this hardware
Left behind
Might take it's toll
And my role
Here
Is not to denigrate
Anyone
But rather to illustrate
To everyone
And maybe to educate
Someone
Who's willing to listen
That over 300 wars
Have happened
Since WWII
And you

Don't even know
How many have died
I could have cried
When I learned
That in combat
It was over 100 million
It brought me to my knees
That twice as many died
Of famine or disease
Brought on by these wars
There are sores
On my soul
Because
I killed some of those people
And I buried
A lot of those bodies
I put them to rest
With all the respect
I could muster
At the time
I covered them with lime
And I covered them with dirt
And I thought
Selfishly
"That's you
Thank fuck
It's not me"

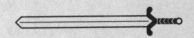

CREATION

The death I see

In my memory

I will never be free

From it

It's a pit

Of sorrow

And I can't borrow

Happiness from anywhere

I live with the pain

The memories

The awful thoughts

Of dust and debris

The screams

And the gore

The blood

And remains

The stains

On my mind

Are permanent

But I'm positive

Because I live

After having
Gone through all of it
My wit
May be bitter at times
Because I have seen things
That most people don't
And I won't
Believe
That anyone
Can understand
Unless they've seen it too
By my hand
I've delivered death
And saved lives
And now I strive
To build things
Because creation brings
Satisfaction

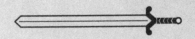

THE END OF WAR

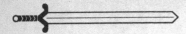

After many nights
Of nightmares
The sun rises
And I stand staring
At the empty street
Beneath
My second story
Windows
Framing
One of the busiest
Intersections
In the city
There are no people
And no cars
And no noise
Only the smoke
From my smoldering cigarette
And the continually cooling
Cup of coffee
In my hand
Are indications

Of the passage of time
It's like
I'm looking at
A photograph
I ponder if this
Is a picture of peace
Is this really
How war will cease?
With no one left
To fight it
I'm fascinated
By this vision
That my mind has cast
But finally
I turn away
Because I know
That it can't last

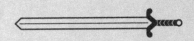

THE BULLET

I didn't feel the bullet
That pierced me
Punctured me
Punched me
And knocked me
To the ground
I found myself
Lying there
Wondering where
In the hell
That came from
I was deaf and dumb
My body
Totally numb
I couldn't hear
And I couldn't scream
All I could do was see
The mayhem
Continue around me
And my blood
Leaking in a runnel

From this funnel
This hole
In my chest
And as it took its' toll
My sight faded
And my jaded
View of the world
Turned to black
And I wonder sometimes
If it will ever come back
To colour

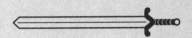

REMEMBRANCE DAY

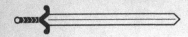

I remember
And I will not forget
I remember
South Sudan
And Vietnam
Khe San
And Dien Bien Phu
I remember
The Congo too
In fact
All of Africa
From A to Z
Angola to Zimbabwe
I remember
Ancient history
Marathon
The sack of Troy
Cannae
Thermopylae
Not far away
From Gergovia

And Alesia
The first and second
Punic War
Then there's
El Salvador
And Nicaraugua
Sri Lanka
And Rwanda
I remember
The 900 days
Of Leningrad
The Winter War
And Stalingrad
Where everyone
Froze their tits
I remember Austerlitz
And the London Blitz
The fire bombing of Dresden
The forest of Ardennes
I remember Borodino
And Sarajevo
And Shiloh
Ghettysburg
And Vicksburg
Fredricksburg
The battles of Bull Run
One and two
And who

Could forget Caizhou
Or Kaifeng
Yehuling
Changping
Or the massacre of Nanking
Gualcanal
Iwo Jima
Hiroshima
And Nagasaki
I remember
Gallipoli
And Prokhorovkie
I remember the end of an age
At Stamford Bridge
Bannockburn
Vimy Ridge
And Passchendale
The Marne
And the Somme
I remember
Crecy
And Agincourt
And Arracourt
And Culloden Moor
Where the Scots
Were not allowed to yield
I remember Bosworth Field
And the siege of Orleans

Tobruk
And El Alamien
And I remember
What I've seen
First hand
It's seared in my mind
By the burning of flares
And all the empty stares
Of the dead
All this and more
Is stuck in my head
The blood and gore
The detritus of war
And all the sacrifice
Of all of those
Who didn't think twice
About stepping into the fray
About giving their lives away
For what they believed
We were soldiers
I remember
And I will not forget

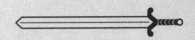

VALHALLA WAITS FOR ME

One night
After a bunch
Of firefights
The lights came on
And I realized
That I wasn't afraid
That I had paid
For my ticket
And my seat
In Valhalla
Was reserved
I would get
What I deserved
If there really is
An afterlife
The strife
That I faced
Has guaranteed
My place
On a bench
In the drinking hall

Of Valhalla
With others like me
At the table
Maybe it's a fable
But I have no fear
Death is always near
And I will never veer
Away from it
No matter
What comes after

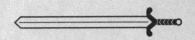

Sticking To My Psyche

Sticking to my psyche
Is the fight
Burnt so bright
In that phosphorous night
With horrors held at bay by dark
Their mark
Awaits the break of day
Show who's to pay
In the devastation wrought
By those who fought
I've sought
Relief from sorrow
In the cleft of peaches
Sunset beaches
Have held
No happiness for me
But I love the look
Of doom and gloom
On a rainy weekend
With all the little houses

Cringing under their little roofs
It behooves me
To appreciate
The lack of recognition
The admition
That comes with suffering
On sun/bloodsoaked ground
I've found
More humanity
Amongst the debris
And torn pieces
In the remains
Whose nieces?
Nephews?
Or children?
Mothers?
Fathers?
Daughters or sons?
Have fallen
To these nocturnal guns?

Sticking to my psyche
Is the sound of passing lead
Whinging
Whining
Cutting thru the air
My hair stands up on end
All over my body
With my pubes uncurled

I fire in retaliation
Make my piece
Work in my defense
I don't know
What I hit or who
Or Even if I do
I don't feel safe
I don't feel unsafe
Why should I?
When I could die
At any moment of the day
Goddamn
Goddamn
Goddamn
What else can I say
When any bullet could find me stray
Like my buddy
Who's body
Lies beside me in the mud
Only a trickle of blood
Is a sign
To define
The lack of life
His glazed eyes
No longer see
What's happening
Around me
The struggle of my soul

In this muddy bloody hole
To love and laugh or cry
To fear and fight or die
In defense of people
I only met a month ago
I didn't know
That I would carry forward
All their faces
To all the future places
Where my rest
Is still disturbed
By the unheard screams
Suppressed
Beneath the blanket of sound
Laid down
In carnal hell
By mortar shells
Machine guns
And small arms fire
Providing a staccato symphony
Throughout the night
The music's beautiful –
If you listen right

Sticking to my psyche
Is the fact that
In the western world
We worry about parking fines
When 100 million land mines

Lie in wait
For unsuspecting children
Playing games
Their names
Are known to those
Who love them
But do we care?
Do we dare?
To think about the consequences
Of the military actions
Interactions
That human beings
Creating conflict
Inflict
With pain and misery
Upon each other
Why
Do
We
Bother
To make believe
It doesn't happen
Shouldn't happen
Or couldn't happen
I happen
To know otherwise
And I know that
Size doesn't matter

When you hit a human
With a .762
The caliber of the lead
Doesn't separate
The living from the dead
Dead
Is how it ends
Unleavened bread
Doesn't separate
AKs from uzis
Nor can M16s
Separate rice from beans
Wheatcakes and nutpaste
Do not a diet make
But I would take
Life in a foreign village
Over contemporary culture
Any day

Sticking to my psyche
Are bits of sparkling earth
Sprinting and spritzing
Towards the sky
Little bits of dirt
That don't belong to day
Their deflections of light
Reserved
For the reflections of night
Under sodium exposure

Those moments in between rounds
The sounds that coincide
With momentary flashes
Of illumination
Epiphanies
Of death
Exposed in its' raw
Pictures of fear
On every face
Every heart
Every soul
Every body subjected
Whether live or not

Sticking to my psyche
Is a burning in the back of head
That makes me think
I might be dead
That I've lost my stake
But when I wake
There's someone
Pulling shrapnel
From my skull
And I recognize
This empty hull
That is my body
Lying in the dirt and detritus
From a battle fought
Throughout the night

Whose right
Was it anyway
To take away these lives
And body parts
To leave these scars
I might
Recover physically
From this experience
But the residue
Sticking to my psyche
Will always
Be with me